Fun with Heat

written by Maria Gordon
and
illustrated by Mike Gordon

Thomson Learning
New York

Simple Science
Float and Sink
Fun with Color
Fun with Heat
Fun with Light

First published in the
United States in 1995 by
Thomson Learning
New York, NY

Published simultaneously in Great Britain by Wayland (Publishers) Limited

Library of Congress Cataloging-in-Publication Data

Gordon, Maria.
  Fun with heat / written by Maria Gordon and
illustrated by Mike Gordon.
         p.   cm. — (Simple science)
  Includes bibliographical references and index.
  ISBN 1-56847-438-5. — ISBN 1-56847-500-4 (pbk.)
  1. Heat—Juvenile literature. 2. Heat—Experiments—
Juvenile literature. [1. Heat—Experiments. 2. Experiments.]
I. Gordon, Mike, ill. II. Title. III. Series: Simple science (New York, N.Y.)
QC271.2.G67   1995
536—dc20   94-46476

Printed in Italy

Contents

Heat is a kind of energy.
It is called energy
because it makes
things happen.

Heat can make soft
things hard and
hard things soft.

Heat is... the warmth of the sun... the feel of hot potatoes... and even the feel of another person!

The sun heats the whole world. But some parts of the world are hotter than others.

The Earth is round. The parts around its center are closest to the sun. They get more heat and are generally hotter.

The sun sends out heat that people, plants, and animals need to live. Heat also comes from volcanoes, hot springs, and lightning.

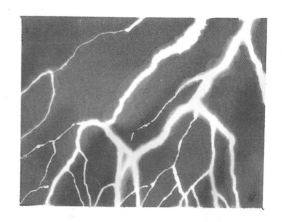

People have found many ways to make heat themselves. How many ways can you see here? How is the heat being used?

Cave people rubbed sticks or struck stones together to make fires from wood.

Fire scared dangerous animals away, kept the people warm, and cooked the people's food.

Later, people learned how to burn oil and coal for cooking and heating.

The Romans even heated houses and swimming pools by sending hot air under floors.

11

You can make heat by friction. This means rubbing things together. Rub your hands together and feel the heat.

You can also make heat using pressure.

Press two ice cubes together. They warm up and melt where they touch. If you stop pressing they freeze again and stick together!

12

Turn on a lamp. Do not touch it, but feel around it. Electricity makes the bulb get hot inside.

Heat is also produced in a compost pile, because heat is made when things decay.

Many things that get very hot mix with air and make fire. This is called burning. Something that burns is called fuel. Wood, coal, oil, gasoline, and natural gas are all fuels.

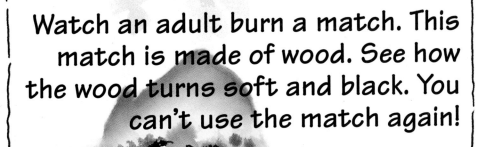

Watch an adult burn a match. This match is made of wood. See how the wood turns soft and black. You can't use the match again!

Fuels can only be used once. We must be careful not to use them all up.

Heat is always moving. It flows from warmer things to cooler things.

Put three bowls on a table. Ask an adult to fill the bowl on your left with cold water and the bowl on your right with hot water. Fill the middle bowl with warm water.

HOT   WARM   COLD

Put your left hand in the cold water for about a minute.

Your hand feels cold because heat flows out of it into the cooler water.

At the same time, put your right hand in the hot water. The heat flows from the water to your hand. Your hand feels hot.

Now put both hands into the middle bowl.
The water feels warm to your left hand, but
cold to your right hand!

Heat is flowing from the water into your left
hand, but it is flowing out of your right
hand and into the water.

Heat flows through some things better than others. Hold a pencil to an ice cube. Your fingers do not feel much different. Heat does not flow well through wood.

Now touch the ice cube with a coin. Your fingers feel very cold. Heat flows through metal very well.

Heat does not flow well through air. Air helps keep things warm.

Wool and fur trap air between their tiny hairs.

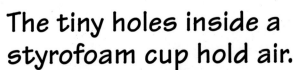

The tiny holes inside a styrofoam cup hold air.

Heat makes many things change. Leave some chocolate on a plate in the sun. Watch the chocolate melt. Heat flows into it.

Put the chocolate in a freezer. The heat flows out of it and it gets hard again.

Ask an adult to help you make some cake batter. Pour the batter into a cake pan and put it in the oven.

The heat from the oven makes the mixture firm.

The cooked cake batter is different from the chocolate. It doesn't change back when it cools down.

Heat makes many things expand. Look at a glass thermometer. The red or silver line in it goes up when it gets warm.

BODY HEAT
98·6°F

This is how a thermometer measures how hot things are. It measures temperature.

FREEZING
32°F

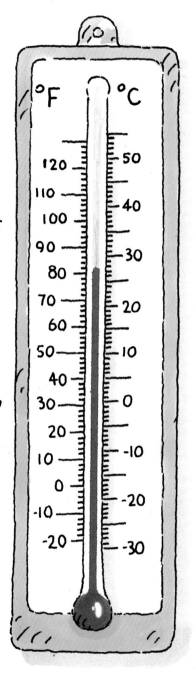

°F   °C

120   50
110
100   40
90   30
80
70   20
60
50   10
40
30   0
20
10   -10
0
-10   -20
-20   -30

Cold things have
low temperatures.

Hot things have
high temperatures.

Ask an adult up to
help you measure the
temperatures of
different things.

The food you eat makes heat inside you. You can die if you get too hot or too cold. If you didn't sweat, you could bake. If you didn't wear clothes, you could freeze.

Animals' bodies have different ways to keep cool or to stay warm. Polar bears would freeze if they didn't have thick fur coats.

But if elephants had fur they would bake. Their enormous ears help them to lose heat.

Seals would shiver without fat beneath their skins.

27

Burning too much fuel in the world makes the air thicker. This makes it hold too much heat.

The extra heat could hurt people, plants, and animals. It could melt the North and South Poles, too. This would make the seas flood and cover the land where people live and plants grow.

One way that we can stop this from happening is by using the sun's heat to make electricity. In sunny places, solar panels are used to make enough electricity to supply houses.

You can also help to save heat energy.

1

2

3

Can you identify these ways of saving heat? The answers are on page 31.

Additional Projects

Here are a few more projects to test out heat. The projects go with the pages listed next to them. These projects are harder than the ones in the book, so be sure to ask an adult to help you.

4/5 Most of the changes in weather have to do with changes in temperature. Find out how changes in temperature cause rain, snow, and wind.

8/9 Make a miniature greenhouse with a glass jar over grass on a lawn. Compare growth with uncovered grass. Visit forges, glassworks, potteries, and greenhouses.

12/13 Feel the heat from a bicycle pump in action. Watch for shooting stars burning because of friction with the atmosphere. Do a safety project on house fires.

14/15 Make a chart showing fuels used at home and school. Find out how fuel is used for other things, such as transportation and factories.

16/17 Feel the side of a refrigerator. Find out why it is warm on the outside but cold on the inside.

20/21 Dark objects soak up light, which makes them absorb warmth, too. Put ice cubes in sunshine under black cloths and white cloths. How much faster does the ice cube under the black cloth melt?

22/23 Read about the three states of matter. Make and bake clay models.

24/25 Heat rises. Hot-air balloons rise because the air inside the balloon is warmed, which makes it lighter than the air outside the balloon. Read about the Montgolfier brothers. Maybe you could take a trip in a balloon!

28/29 Make a display of sun safety items such as sun block, parasols, and sunglasses. Find out why is it so important to protect yourself from the sun. Investigate unusual means of keeping things warm; for example, heat from rabbits in hutches has been used for greenhouses!

Answers

1. Turn off unneeded radiators or other heaters.
2. Wear sweaters or sweatshirts to keep warm so you can lower the heat.
3. Fiberglass insulation in attics helps keep heat in the house.

Other books to read

Charman, Andrew. **Fire.** First Starts. Milwaukee: Raintree Steck-Vaughn, 1994.

Gordon, Maria. **Fun with Light.** Simple Science. New York: Thomson Learning, 1995.

Parker, Steve. **Keeping Cool: How You Sweat, Shiver and Keep Warm.** The Body in Action. New York: Franklin Watts, 1992.

Richardson, Joy. **Heat.** Picture Science. New York: Franklin Watts, 1993.

Index